ONE STEP AT A TIME

BEGINNERS GUIDE TO

LINEAR

DRUMMING

Dedicated to
Caroline Maitland

Recorded at 121 Drum school
Sound Engineer: Alan Wall

A special thanks to my good friend Michael A Scott for his advice, encouragement and words of wisdom.

INTRODUCTION

Throughout the years I have been teaching, many of my students have asked me to teach them linear grooves. As a result, I decided to write out exercises that would give a full understanding of what the concept of linear drumming was, and that even the absolute beginner could play. This book is a collection of those exercises which increase in difficulty as you progress through the sections. The exercises begin with simple ¼ note patterns leading up to fully orchestrated 1/16th note linear grooves and fills taking you to an intermediate level.

WHAT IS LINEAR DRUMMING?

The Linear drumming concept is when no two limbs play at the same time. Each drum or cymbal is played separately. It is basically the opposite of playing in unison; which means two or more drums being played at the same time.

Here is an example of a typical eighth note groove played in unison (not Linear)

Example of linear (one drum played at a time)

This style of playing can really open up new possibilities of rhythmic patterns and musical expression. To hear some linear playing in action check out the classic Paul Simon record 50 Ways to Leave Your Lover. The groove is played by one of my inspirations Steve Gadd. Also check out Tower of Power with drummer David Garibaldi laying down some funky linear grooves.

The main aim of this book is to enable you to play 1/16th note linear grooves and Fills. The easy step by step layout of this book will make it possible for even the absolute beginner drummer, with proper practice, to play some really nice linear grooves and fills on completion of all sections.
This book is also suitable for any drummer who is new to this concept of playing and wants to broaden their vocabulary, technique, co ordination and musical expression.

How to use this book

When working through the exercises it is very important to repeat each line until you can play it with ease before moving on. Each note has to be accurately placed and I **strongly recommend** practicing everything in this book with a metronome. Don't rush through it, take your time. The more you repeat each pattern the easier the next one will be. The sticking patterns are all written out for you but feel free to adapt them once you have mastered the examples shown.

Sticking pattern means which hand will play each note R = Right hand L = Left hand
Example RLRL and adapted could be RLLR

Free audio examples of exercises and grooves marked (mp3) in this book are available to download at www.thedrumbook.com

Simply go to **www.thedrumbook.com/downloads**
Username: guest
Password: linear77

Drum notation key

1. Bass Drum
2. Floor Tom
3. Snare Drum
4. Mid Tom
5. Hi Tom
6. Hi Hat closed
7. Hi Hat with foot

How to count the Rhythms

Quarter notes

Eighth notes

Sixteenth notes

SECTION 1

In this first section we will look at quarter note exercises and eighth note exercises. Each exercise is split into two parts, A and B.

Part A is played between the Bass drum and Snare drum and part B is played by using the exact same pattern but simply moving your right hand onto the hi hat. Pay attention to the sticking patterns as many of these exercises will require you to play a double stroke RR rather than just RL.

When playing part A exercises, make sure both sticks are played from the same height to produce an even volume between right and left hand. Each exercise should be repeated at the very least 4 times. Once you have finished with an exercise it is a good idea to play it again starting with the opposite hand, for example RLR would become LRL. This will help strengthen your weak side and open up more creative possibilities. Play each exercise with a strict tempo marking using a metronome. Start slowly and increase the tempo as you become familiar with each exercise. Remember it is not speed we are trying to achieve here but accuracy of each note placement.

QUARTER NOTES

Exercise 1A (mp3)

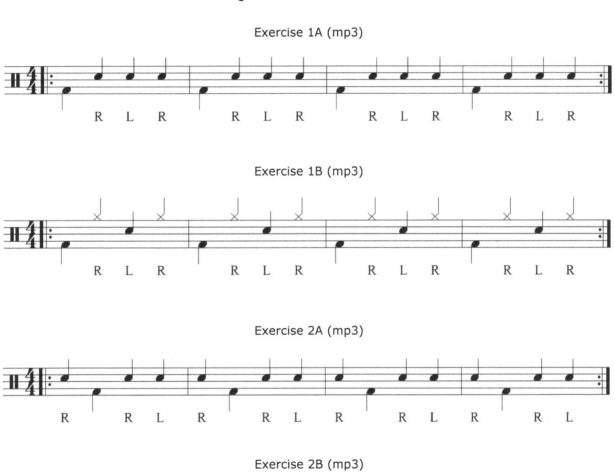

Exercise 1B (mp3)

Exercise 2A (mp3)

Exercise 2B (mp3)

Exercise 3A (mp3)

Exercise 3B (mp3)

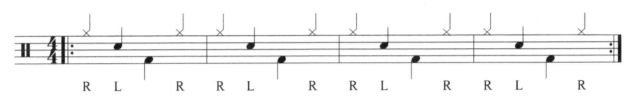

Exercise 4A (mp3)

Exercise 4B (mp3)

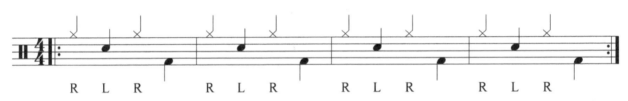

Exercise 5A (mp3)

Exercise 5B (mp3)

Exercise 6A (mp3)

R   L   R   L   R   L   R   L

Exercise 6B (mp3)

R   L   R   L   R   L   R   L

Exercise 7A (mp3)

R   L   R   L   R   L   R   L

Exercise 7B (mp3)

R   L   R   L   R   L   R   L

Exercise 8A (mp3)

R   L   R   L   R   L   R   L

Exercise 8B (mp3)

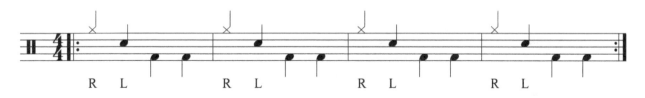

R   L   R   L   R   L   R   L

EIGHTH NOTES

Now we will continue the same steps but this time using eighth notes. Again part A is played between the Bass drum and Snare drum and part B is played by moving your right hand onto the Hi Hat.

Exercise 9A (mp3)

R L R L R L R   R L R L R L R   R L R L R L R   R L R L R L R

Exercise 9B (mp3)

R L R L R L R   R L R L R L R   R L R L R L R   R L R L R L R

Exercise 10A (mp3)

R   R L R L R L   R   R L R L R L   R   R L R L R L   R   R L R L R L

Exercise 10B (mp3)

R   R L R L R L   R   R L R L R L   R   R L R L R L   R   R L R L R L

Exercise 11A (mp3)

R L   R L R L R   R L   R L R L R   R L   R L R L R   R L   R L R L R

Exercise 11B (mp3)

R L   R L R L R   R L   R L R L R   R L   R L R L R   R L   R L R L R

Exercise 12A (mp3)

R L R   R L R L   R L R   R L R L   R L R   R L R L   R L R   R L R L

Exercise 12B (mp3)

R L R   R L R L   R L R   R L R L   R L R   R L R L   R L R   R L R L

Exercise13A

R L R L   R L R   R L R L   R L R   R L R L   R L R   R L R L   R L R

Exercise 13B

R L R L   R L R   R L R L   R L R   R L R L   R L R   R L R L   R L R

Exercise 14A

R L R L R   R L   R L R L R   R L   R L R L R   R L   R L R L R   R L

Exercise 14B

R L R L R   R L   R L R L R   R L   R L R L R   R L   R L R L R   R L

Exercise 15A

R L R L R L   R   R L R L R L   R   R L R L R L   R   R L R L R L   R

Exercise 15B

R L R L R L   R   R L R L R L   R   R L R L R L   R   R L R L R L   R

Exercise 16A

R L R L R L R   R L R L R L R   R L R L R L R   R L R L R L R

Exercise 16B

R L R L R L R   R L R L R L R   R L R L R L R   R L R L R L R

Exercise 17A (mp3)

R L R L R L   R L R L R L   R L R L R L   R L R L R L

Exercise 17B (mp3)

R L R L R L   R L R L R L   R L R L R L   R L R L R L

Exercise 18A (mp3)

R R L R L R R R L R L R R R L R L R R R L R L R

Exercise 18B (mp3)

R R L R L R R R L R L R R R L R L R R R L R L R

Exercise 19A (mp3)

R L R L R L R L R L R L R L R L R L R L R L R L

Exercise 19B (mp3)

R L R L R L R L R L R L R L R L R L R L R L R L

Exercise 20A (mp3)

R L R R L R R L R R L R R L R R L R R L R R L R

Exercise 20B (mp3)

R L R R L R R L R R L R R L R R L R R L R R L R

Exercise 21A

RLRL RL RLRL RL RLRL RL RLRL RL

Exercise 21B

RLRL RL RLRL RL RLRL RL RLRL RL

Exercise 22A

RLRLR L RLRLR L RLRLR L RLRLR L

Exercise 22B

RLRLR L RLRLR L RLRLR L RLRLR L

Exercise 23A

RLRLRL RLRLRL RLRLRL RLRLRL

Exercise 23B

RLRLRL RLRLRL RLRLRL RLRLRL

Exercise 24A (mp3)

R   RLRLR   R   RLRLR   R   RLRLR   R   RLRLR

Exercise 24B (mp3)

R   RLRLR   R   RLRLR   R   RLRLR   R   RLRLR

Exercise 25A (mp3)

R   L   RLRL R   L   RLRL R   L   RLRL R   L   RLRL

Exercise 25B (mp3)

R   L   RLRL R   L   RLRL R   L   RLRL R   L   RLRL

Exercise 26A

RL   R   RLR RL   R   RLR RL   R   RLR RL   R   RLR

Exercise 26B

RL   R   RLR RL   R   RLR RL   R   RLR RL   R   RLR

Exercise 27A

R L R R R L R L R R R L R L R R R L R L R R R L

Exercise 27B

R L R R R L R L R R R L R L R R R L R L R R R L

Exercise 28A

R L R L R R R L R L R R R L R L R R R L R L R R

Exercise 28B

R L R L R R R L R L R R R L R L R R R L R L R R

Exercise 29A

R L R L R R R L R L R R R L R L R R R L R L R R

Exercise 29B

R L R L R R R L R L R R R L R L R R R L R L R R

SECTION 2

In this section we will now play the exercises using sixteenth notes. We will use the same steps as before but this time we have introduced a new exercise by playing accents with the left hand on the snare drum.

Accents are notes that are played louder relative to the other notes. Try not to think of hitting the drum harder but think in terms of lifting your stick higher to create the louder note whilst staying relaxed. This gives the groove dynamics. A lot of Western music has a backbeat on 2 and 4 in each bar; however, not all musical styles use a 2 and 4 backbeat. For example, we can use linear grooves in styles such as Latin, Funk and Fusion and the following exercises will help you play accents in different places in the phrasing. This allows you to develop sixteenth note linear patterns whilst improving your technique, vocabulary, coordination and timing.

Exercise A is played between Bass drum and Snare drum without accents. Exercise B is played between the Bass drum and Snare drum with left hand accents on the Snare. In exercise C, the right hand plays the Hi-Hat. When playing exercise C, use the tip of the stick on the middle of the Hi-Hats. When playing the unaccented notes on the snare drum keep your stick approx. 1" from the drum to give a quieter tone. To play the accents on the Snare, I would recommend using rim shots (hitting the rim and centre of the Snare at the same time) as this creates a big dynamic range. It's this difference in volume that makes these patterns 'groove'.

Again it is very important to play along with a metronome and repeat each pattern until you can play it with ease

SIXTEENTH NOTE

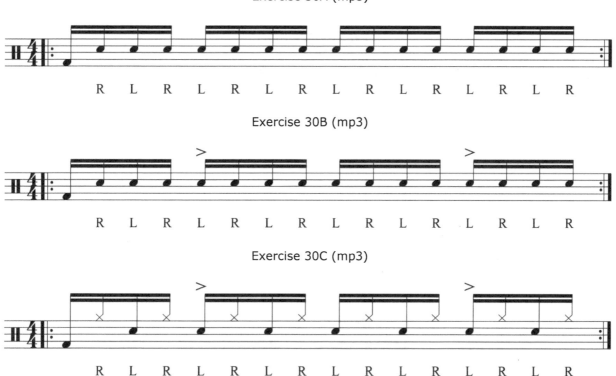

Exercise 31A (mp3)

R   R L R L R L R L R L R L R L

Exercise 31B (mp3)

R   R L R L R L R L R L R L R L

Exercise 31C (mp3)

R   R L R L R L R L R L R L R L

Exercise 32A (mp3)

R L   R L R L R L R L R L R L R

Exercise 32B (mp3)

R L   R L R L R L R L R L R L R

Exercise 32C (mp3)

R L   R L R L R L R L R L R L R

Exercise 33A (mp3)

R L R R L R L R L R L R L R L

Exercise 33B (mp3)

R L R R L R L R L R L R L R L

Exercise 33C (mp3)

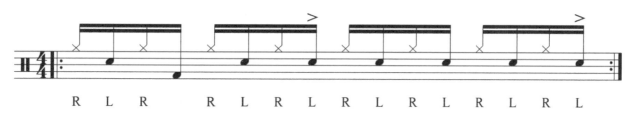

R L R R L R L R L R L R L R L

Exercise 34A

R L R L R L R L R L R L R L R

Exercise 34B

R L R L R L R L R L R L R L R

Exercise 34C

R L R L R L R L R L R L R L R

Exercise 35A

R L R L R   R L R L R L R L R L

Exercise 35B

R L R L R   R L R L R L R L R L

Exercise 35C

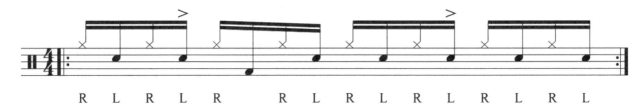

R L R L R   R L R L R L R L R L

Exercise 36A

R L R L R L   R L R L R L R L R

Exercise 36B

R L R L R L   R L R L R L R L R

Exercise 36C

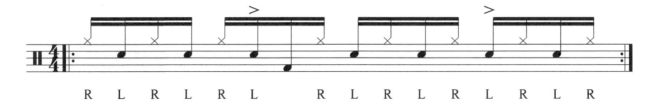

R L R L R L   R L R L R L R L R

Exercise 37A

Exercise 37B

Exercise 37C

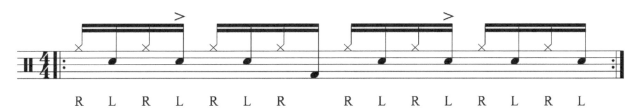

Exercise 38A

Exercise 38B

Exercise 38C

Exercise 39A

R L R L R L R L   R L R L R L

Exercise 39B

R L R L R L R L   R L R L R L

Exercise 39C

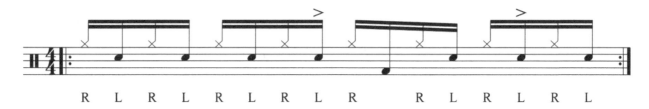

R L R L R L R L R   R L R L R L

Exercise 40A

R L R L R L R L R L   R L R L R

Exercise 40B

R L R L R L R L R L   R L R L R

Exercise 40C

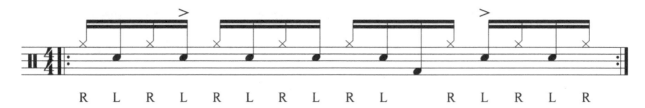

R L R L R L R L R L   R L R L R

Exercise 41A

R L R L R L R L R L R   R L R L

Exercise 41B

R L R L R L R L R L R   R L R L

Exercise 41C

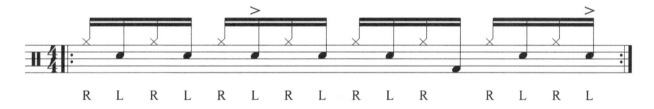

R L R L R L R L R L R   R L R L

Exercise 42A

R L R L R L R L R L R L   R L R

Exercise 42B

R L R L R L R L R L R L   R L R

Exercise 42C

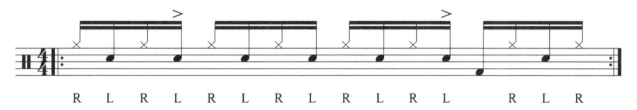

R L R L R L R L R L R L   R L R

Exercise 43A

R   L   R   L   R   L   R   L   R   L   R   L   R   R   L

Exercise 43B

R   L   R   L   R   L   R   L   R   L   R   L   R   R   L

Exercise 43C

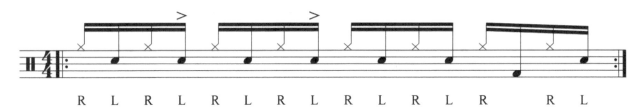

R   L   R   L   R   L   R   L   R   L   R   L   R   R   L

Exercise 44A

R   L   R   L   R   L   R   L   R   L   R   L   R   L   L

Exercise 44B

R   L   R   L   R   L   R   L   R   L   R   L   R   L   L

Exercise 44C

R   L   R   L   R   L   R   L   R   L   R   L   R   L   L

Exercise 45A

R L R L R L R L R L R L R L R L

Exercise 45B

R L R L R L R L R L R L R L R L

Exercise 45C

R L R L R L R L R L R L R L R L

Exercise 46A (mp3)

R L R L R L R L R L R L R L R L

Exercise 46B (mp3)

R L R L R L R L R L R L R L R L

Exercise 46C (mp3)

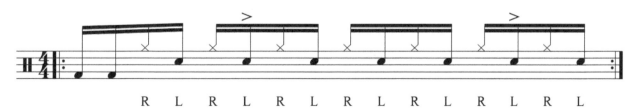

R L R L R L R L R L R L R L R L

Exercise 47A (mp3)

R   R L R L R L R L R L R L R

Exercise 47B (mp3)

R   R L R L R L R L R L R L R

Exercise 47C (mp3)

R   R L R L R L R L R L R L R

Exercise 48A (mp3)

R L   R L R L R L R L R L R L

Exercise 48B (mp3)

R L   R L R L R L R L R L R L

Exercise 48C (mp3)

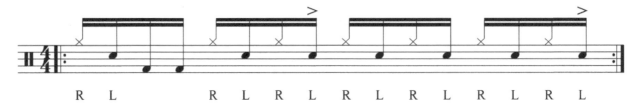

R L   R L R L R L R L R L R L

25

Exercise 49A (mp3)

Exercise 49B (mp3)

Exercise 49C (mp3)

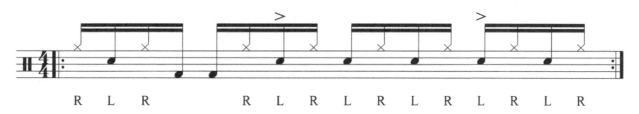

Exercise 50A

Exercise 50B

Exercise 50C

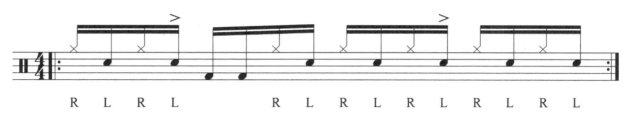

Exercise 51A

R L R L R   R L R L R L R L R

Exercise 51B

R L R L R   R L R L R L R L R

Exercise 51C

R L R L R   R L R L R L R L R

Exercise 52A

R L R L R L   R L R L R L R L

Exercise 52B

R L R L R L   R L R L R L R L

Exercise 52C

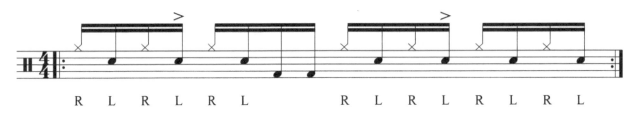

R L R L R L   R L R L R L R L

Exercise 53A

R L R L R L R   R L R L R L R

Exercise 53B

R L R L R L R   R L R L R L R

Exercise 53C

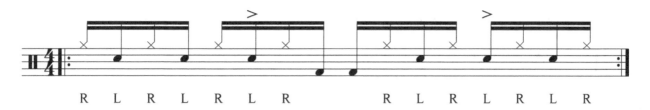

R L R L R L R   R L R L R L R

Exercise 54A

R L R L R L R L   R L R L R L

Exercise 54B

R L R L R L R L   R L R L R L

Exercise 54C

R L R L R L R L   R L R L R L

Exercise 55A

R L R L R L R L R   R L R L R

Exercise 55B

R L R L R L R L R   R L R L R

Exercise 55C

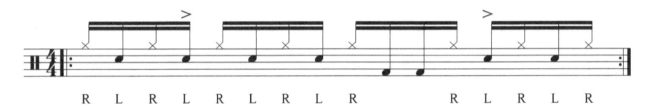

R L R L R L R L R   R L R L R

Exercise 56A

R L R L R L R L R L   R L R L

Exercise 56B

R L R L R L R L R L   R L R L

Exercise 56C

R L R L R L R L R L   R L R L

29

Exercise 57A

R L R L R L R L R L R R L R

Exercise 57B

R L R L R L R L R L R R L R

Exercise 57C

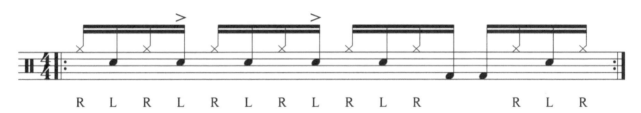

R L R L R L R L R L R R L R

Exercise 58A

R L R L R L R L R L R L R L

Exercise 58B

R L R L R L R L R L R L R L

Exercise 58C

R L R L R L R L R L R L R L

Exercise 59A

R L R L R L R L R L R L R L

Exercise 59B

R L R L R L R L R L R L R L

Exercise 59C

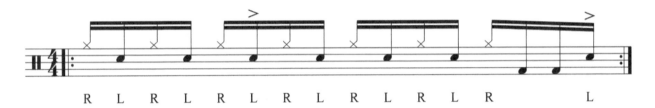

R L R L R L R L R L R L R L

Exercise 60A

R L R L R L R L R L R L R L

Exercise 60B

R L R L R L R L R L R L R L

Exercise 60C

R L R L R L R L R L R L R L

Exercise 61A

R　L　R　L　R　L　R　L　R　L　R　L　R　L

Exercise 61B

R　L　R　L　R　L　R　L　R　L　R　L　R　L

Exercise 61C

R　L　R　L　R　L　R　L　R　L　R　L　R　L

What you have achieved so far.

Now you can play 1/4 notes, 1/8th notes and 1/16th notes between the Bass drum, Snare drum and Hi- Hats with accents on the Snare.
Remember to play each exercise again starting with your left hand.

SECTION 3

This section now introduces 1/16th note grooves using a mixture of the previous exercises. Let's use part C of the previous 1/16th note exercises 30 to 61.

If we take different sections from those exercises and put them together we can construct some nice grooves and ideas. The following examples use the C parts from the exercises but feel free to add in any part you want. The idea is to be creative and think musically.

SIXTEENTH NOTE GROOVES

If we take the first 8 notes of exercise 30C we have this

R   L   R   L   R   L   R

If we then take the last 8 notes of exercise 39C we have this

R   R   L   R   L   R   L

Now put the two together to create a full bar linear groove with snare drum accents

Groove example 1A

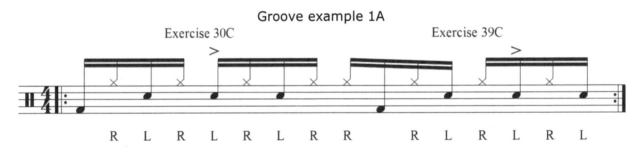

R   L   R   L   R   L   R   R   R   L   R   L   R   L

To add an extra feel to the groove we can add in Hi-Hat accents. Since you have been using the tip of the stick to play the Hi-Hat, we will use the shoulder of the stick on the edge of the Hi-Hat to produce this accent. This can be quite tricky so I would suggest playing them at a slow tempo until you get used to the stroke motion. If you have a drum teacher he/she will go through these motions with you.

Combined exercises with Snare Drum and Hi Hat accents.

Groove example 1B

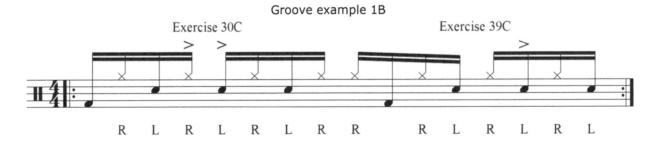

R   L   R   L   R   L   R   R   R   L   R   L   R   L

Next example takes the first 8 notes of exercise 34C and the last 8 notes of exercise 40C

Groove example 2A (mp3)

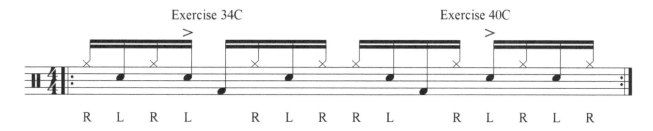

Now add in Hi-Hat accents

Groove example 2B (mp3)

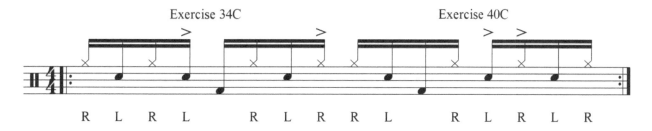

Next example takes the first 8 notes of exercise 32C and the last 8 notes of 41C

Groove example 3A (mp3)

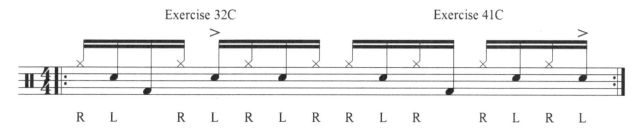

With added Hi-Hat accents

Groove example 3B (mp3)

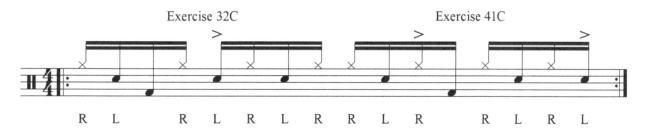

There is so much we can do with these exercises and grooves. Let's take the above example. We could simply repeat the first 8 notes to create a new groove. Or we could just play the last 8 notes and repeat them or even reverse the order so you would have exercise 41C then exercise 32C.

Experiment around and remember to be creative. Here are more examples of combining the previous exercises.

This time let's use 3 different previous exercises to construct a groove. Let's take the first 8 notes of exercise 49C

The third 4 notes of Exercise 39C

The last 4 notes of Exercise 59C

We now have this groove

Groove example 4A (mp3)

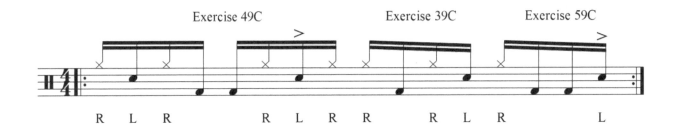

With added Hi-Hat accents

Groove example 4B (mp3)

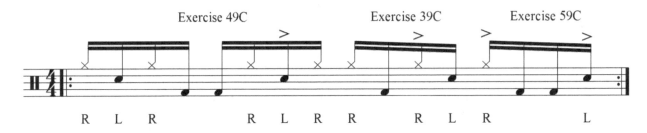

The next example uses 4 different exercises

The first 4 notes of exercise 31C   Second 4 notes of exercise 39C

The third 4 notes of exercise 55C   The last 4 notes of exercise 60C

We now have this groove

Groove example 5A (mp3)

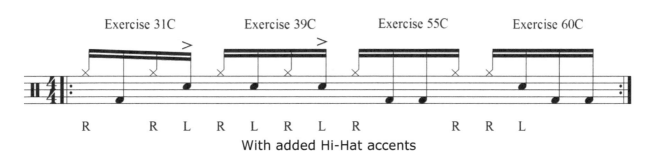

With added Hi-Hat accents

Groove example 5B (mp3)

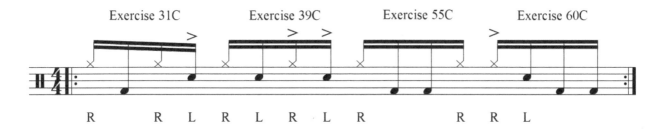

Use the blank manuscript paper on the following pages to write your own grooves using the previous exercises.

Mix up any exercise you want, be creative.

SIXTEENTH NOTE PHRASING

When playing linear grooves in 1/16th notes there are 16 permutations which simply mean 16 places where we can place a note in the bar. We can then put combinations of notes together to add up to 16. For example 3 notes plus 5 notes plus another 3 notes plus another 5 equals 16 notes.

$$3 + 5 + 3 + 5 = 16$$

These combinations are called groupings and really take the linear concept to a new level of playing. By now you should be getting more comfortable with the dynamics required to make these grooves sound the best they can be. The same techniques apply to the following examples.

The groupings used here will be

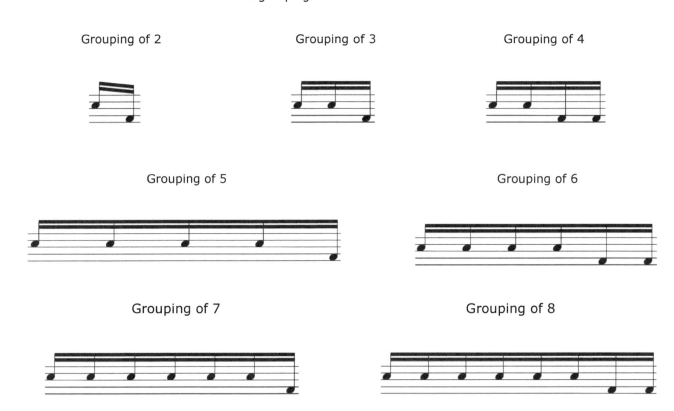

Grouping of 2   Grouping of 3   Grouping of 4

Grouping of 5   Grouping of 6

Grouping of 7   Grouping of 8

Let's take the grouping example above of 3/5/3/5.

We now have this 16th note phrase

Group 1A (mp3)

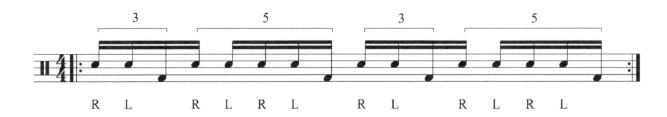

We know to add in Snare drum accents and right hand playing the Hi-Hat just the same way we have previously been doing, so here is the phrase with those added

Group 1B (mp3)

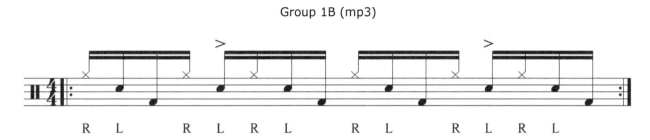

Pretty nice groove right? Let's take it a step further and start orchestrating. Basically we will play the same pattern but this time we can pick out certain notes to play on a different voice.
The following example has moved some right hand Hi Hat parts to the toms

Group 1C (mp3)

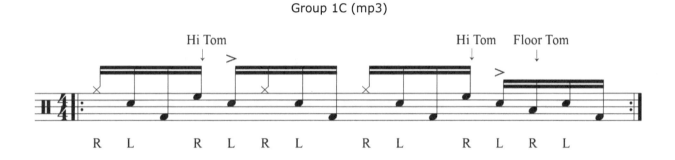

Now let's add in the Hi-Hat with the left foot, commonly called stepped Hi Hat. A good place to start with this technique is to substitute a Bass drum for a stepped Hi Hat

So now we have the original 1/16th note phrase with accents on the Snare, right hand playing the Hi Hat, orchestration and stepped Hi Hat.

Group 1D (mp3)

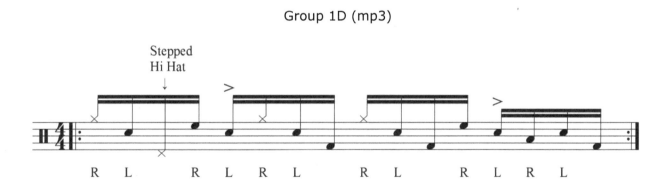

It may take a while to master these new techniques and to have the unaccented notes quiet and the accents loud. Just practice slowly with a metronome until you are comfortable with the grooves and then increase your tempo by 5 bpm. Repeat the process

Group A - Snare drum/Bass drum pattern
Group B – Accents on snare/ Right hand on Hi Hat
Group C – Orchestration
Group D – Stepped Hi Hat

The next example uses groupings 5/3/3/3/2

Group 2A (mp3)

Snare/bass drum phrase

Group 2B (mp3)

Right hand Hi Hat-Snare accents

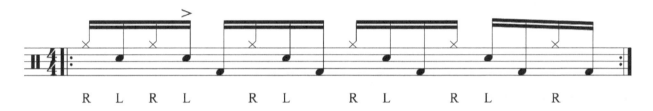

Group 2C (mp3)

Orchestration

Group 2D (mp3)

Stepped Hi Hat

Next example uses groupings 3/6/3/4

Group 3A (mp3)

Snare/bass drum phrase

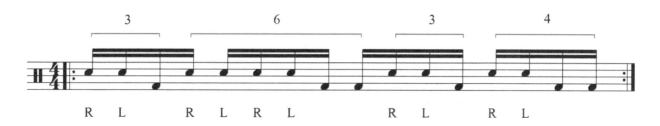

Group 3B (mp3)

Right Hand Hi Hat- Snare accents

Group 3C (mp3)

Orchestration

Group 3D (mp3)

Stepped Hi Hat

Next example uses groupings 4/7/5

Group 4A (mp3)

Snare/bass drum phrase

Group 4B (mp3)

Right hand Hi Hat-Snare accents

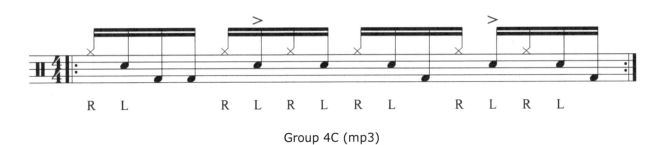

Group 4C (mp3)

Orchestration

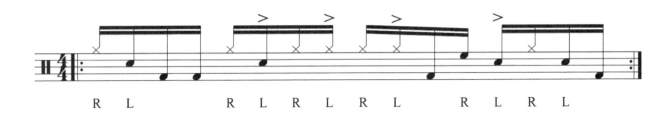

Group 4D (mp3)

Stepped Hi Hat

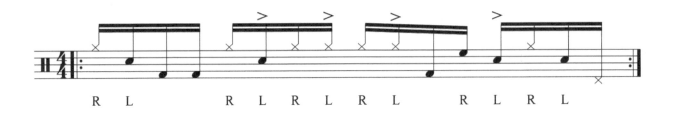

We can also play grooves over 2 or more bars and use these groupings to play over a bar line. The next example uses groupings 3/6/5/5/4/3/3/3 which adds up to 32, and that is 2 bars of 16th notes. Notice how the phrasing runs over the bar line.

Group 5A (mp3)

Snare/bass drum phrase

Group 5B (mp3)

Right hand Hi Hat – Snare accents

Group 5C (mp3)

Orchestration

Group 5D (mp3)

Stepped Hi Hat

FILLS

Here are some linear fill ideas using sixteenth notes. These examples are shown with a straight eighth note groove. Try playing linear grooves and linear fills together and then play straight grooves in unison with linear fills.

Fill 1A (mp3)

R L R   L R L   R L R   L R L

Here is the same fill in context with a straight eighth note groove

Fill 1B (mp3)

Unison   Linear

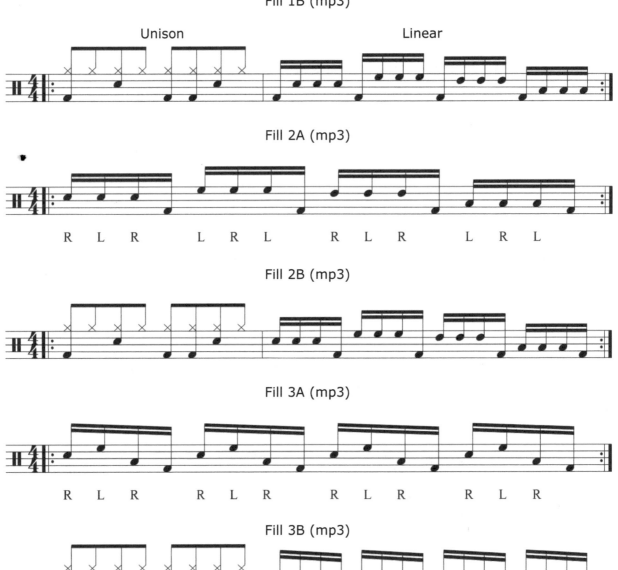

Fill 2A (mp3)

R L R   L R L   R L R   L R L

Fill 2B (mp3)

Fill 3A (mp3)

R L R   R L R   R L R   R L R

Fill 3B (mp3)

The next fill is basically the same as before in terms of phrasing and sticking pattern. The difference is in the orchestration. On the second and fourth beat the pattern has changed slightly.

Fill 4A (mp3)

Fill 4B (mp3)

Fill 5A (mp3)

Fill 5B (mp3)

Fill 6A (mp3)

Fill 6B (mp3)

PHRASING IN FILLS

Just as we done before with the linear groove phrasings using different groupings, we can apply the same concept with fills. Let's take the same groupings as before as examples. The first grouping was 3/5/3/5

Now let's orchestrate that phrase around the drums.

Fill 7A (mp3)

And here is the fill with a straight eighth note groove

Fill 7B (mp3)

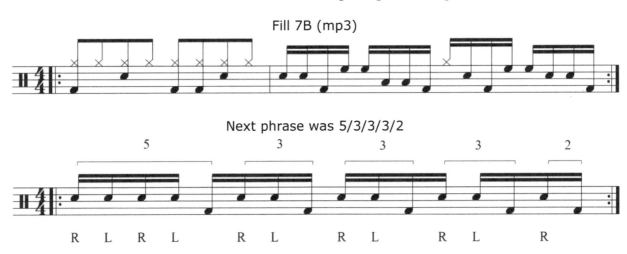

Next phrase was 5/3/3/3/2

Orchestrated around the drums

Fill 8A   Notice the change in sticking

Fill 8B

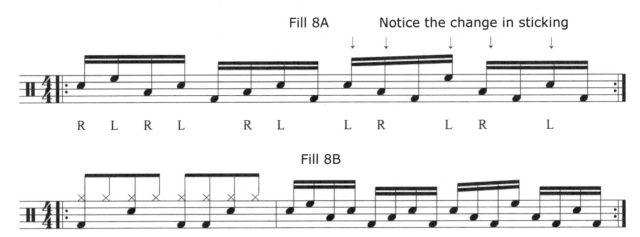

Next example 3/6/3/4

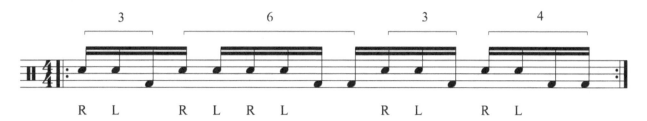

Orchestrated around the drums

Fill 9A

Fill 9B

Next example 4/7/5

Orchestrated around the drums

Fill 10A (mp3)

Fill 10B (mp3)

And the final example was using the groupings over two bars. The grouping was 3/6/5/5/4/3/3/3

Orchestrated around the drums

Fill 11A (mp3)

And again played in context with a straight eighth note groove

Fill 11B (mp3)

Try different groupings, mix up the sticking patterns, start with your weak hand, turn the patterns around and play them backwards, play the patterns on the rims of the drums, hit cymbals instead of toms. Basically what I'm saying here is experiment. There really are no rules maybe just guidelines but music is the expression of emotion, express yourself and most of all have fun in the process.

Use the blank manuscript on the following pages to create your own groupings, grooves and fills.

FURTHER STUDY

For further study try out these ideas.

Play through the same steps as before but using eighth note triplets

Sextuplets

Swung eighth notes (shuffle)

Start on a different permutation. Let's take this groove as an example

Start on a different note and use that as 1

You would now have this groove

Made in United States
Troutdale, OR
11/16/2024

24886376R00031